Flashing Fireflies

by Laura Hamilton Waxman

first step nonfiction

Lerner Publications ◆ Minneapolis

LERNER
SOURCE

Expand learning beyond the printed book. Download free, complementary educational resources for this book from our website, www.lernerresource.com.

The images in this book are used with the permission of: © iStockphoto.com/ABDESIGN, p. 4; © iStockphoto.com/andipantz, p. 5; © James Robinson/Animals Animals, p. 6; © Dwight Kuhn, pp. 7, 9, 13, 15, 17; © Adam Jones/DanitaDelimont.com/Newscom, p. 8; © Phil Degginger/Animals Animals, p. 10; © amana images inc./Alamy, p. 11; © Satoshi Kuribayashi/Minden Pictures, p. 12; © James E Lloyd/Animals Animals, p. 14; © Sdbower/Dreamstime.com, p. 16; © Dale Darwin/Science Source, p. 18; © Floris van Breugel/naturepl.com/Alamy, p. 19; AP Photo/Knoxville News Sentinel/ Adam Lau, p. 20; © Steven Puetzer/Getty Images, p. 21; © Ken Barber/Alamy, p. 22. Front cover: © Dale Darwin/Science Source/Getty Images.

Main body text set in ITC Avant Garde Gothic Std Medium 21/25. Typeface provided by International Typeface Corp.

Lerner Publications Company
A division of Lerner Publishing Group, Inc.
241 First Avenue North
Minneapolis, MN 55401 USA

For reading levels and more information, look up this title at www.lernerbooks.com.

Library of Congress Cataloging-in-Publication Data

Names: Waxman, Laura Hamilton, author.
Title: Flashing fireflies / by Laura Hamilton Waxman.
Description: Minneapolis : Lerner Publications, [2016] | Series: First step nonfiction. Backyard critters | Audience: Ages 5–8. | Audience: K to grade 3. | Includes index.
Identifiers: LCCN 2015036117| ISBN 9781512408829 (lb : alk. paper) | ISBN 9781512412215 (pb : alk. paper) | ISBN 9781512410020 (eb pdf)
Subjects: LCSH: Fireflies—Juvenile literature.
Classification: LCC QL596.L28 W39 2016 | DDC 595.76/44—dc23
LC record available at http://lccn.loc.gov/2015036117

Manufactured in the United States of America
1 – CG – 7/15/16

Table of Contents

Firefly Bodies

Fireflies are brown or black **insects**.

They have flat, oval bodies.

Fireflies have six legs.

Fireflies use their antennae to smell, taste, and touch.

They have two **antennae**.

Fireflies have hard wing covers.

Fireflies are not flies.
They are beetles.

Thin wings for flying are below the covers.

9

Where to Find Fireflies

Fireflies often show up in summer.

These yellow streaks are flying fireflies.

They live in warm, **damp** places.

Fireflies climb up grass to look around.

Many fireflies live in tall grass near water.

No one knows for sure what grown fireflies eat.

13

Most fireflies probably eat
food from flowers.

Fireflies live for only a few days or weeks. They need little to no food.

Some may eat nothing at all.

Snails like this one are a common food for young fireflies.

Young fireflies eat snails, slugs, and small insects.

They kill their food with a shot of **poison**.

Fireflies make light in their **abdomen**.

They flash the light on and off.

Fireflies start lighting up after the sun goes down.

Other fireflies see the flashing.

It tells fireflies where to find
one another.

Firefly Parts

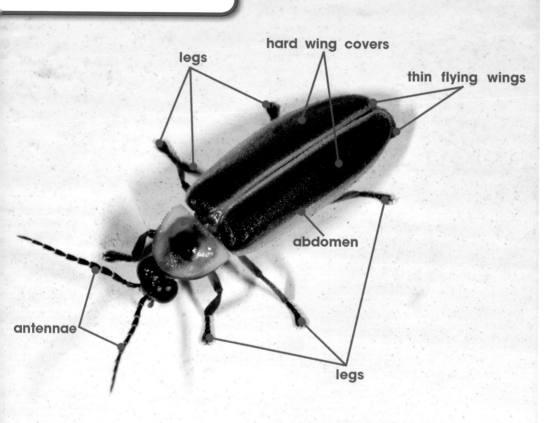

legs

hard wing covers

thin flying wings

abdomen

antennae

legs

Glossary

abdomen – the rear part of an insect's body

antennae – long, thin body parts that stick out of an insect's head

damp – a little wet

insects – small animals with six legs. Insects also often have wings.

poison – something that makes a living thing get sick or die

Index